Rubens

SPRING ART BOOKS

Edward Lucie-Smith

SPRING BOOKS • LONDON

ACKNOWLEDGMENTS

The paintings in this volume are reproduced by kind permission of the following collections, galleries and museums to which they belong: Bayerische Staatsgemäldesammlungen, Munich (Plates II, X, XI, XXXI); National Gallery, London (Plates III, XVII, XXIII, XXV, XXVI, XXXVII–XXXIX, XLI, XLIV, XLVI); Courtauld Institute of Art, London (Plate IV); Royal Museum of Fine Arts, Brussels (Plate V); Art Gallery and Museum, Glasgow (Plate VI); Wallace Collection, London (Plates VII, IX, XV, XVI, XL); Fitzwilliam Museum, Cambridge (Plate VIII); Museum of Fine Arts, Antwerp (Plates XII, XIII, XLVII); National Gallery, Prague (Plates XIV, XLV); Louvre, Paris (Plates XVIII–XXI, XXXII, XLII, XLIII); Kunsthistorisches Museum, Vienna (Plates XXIV, XLVIII); Private Collection, Worcestershire (Plate XXVII); The National Trust (Plates XXXIII, XXXIV); M. Ulysse Moussalli, Paris (Plate XXII). The four details from the *Whitehall Ceiling* (Plates XXVIII–XXX) are reproduced by courtesy of The Ministry of Works, London, and the frontispiece drawing, *Selfportrait*, by courtesy of the Kunsthistorisches Museum, Vienna. The paintings reproduced on Plates V, XVIII–XXII, XXXI, XXXII, XLII, XLIII were photographed by Photographie Giraudon, Paris.

1st Edition 1961

Revised Reprint 1962

2nd Impression 1963

3rd Impression 1964

Published by

SPRING BOOKS

Westbook House · Fulham Broadway · London

© Paul Hamlyn Ltd 1961

Printed in Czechoslovakia

1348

Contents

Introduction

RUBENS has always been one of the very greatest names in European painting. His work has never sunk into obscurity, and it has never been truly out of fashion. Yet, for all this, Rubens never seems to have won the sort of whole-hearted acceptance from his audience which has now been achieved by Rembrandt, by Michelangelo, even by Vermeer.

This uneasiness expresses itself in different ways. One of the commonest and crudest—yet perhaps the most heartfelt—is the cry of 'Oh, all that pink flesh; all those fat nudes!' which is heard so often when Rubens's name is mentioned. But even art lovers who fully acknowledge Rubens's greatness will admit to a certain resistance. They find it less easy to 'fall in love with' his pictures than with those of any other master of comparable stature. He makes his impact, but he never quite conquers; somewhere, somehow, there remains a doubt.

It is not easy to explain such a painter. Rubens's pictures offer an experience which will differ somewhat for every spectator. It is an experience which it is not always easy to describe or to evaluate. The purpose of this introduction is simply to set up a few pointers, to offer signposts towards this; to indicate what can be found in Rubens's enormous *oeuvre*, and what cannot.

Rubens's Early Life

Rubens, the head of the Flemish School, was not born in Flanders at all. He was born, in fact, at Siegen in Westphalia. The date was June 28th, 1577. However, Rubens's parentage was Flemish enough. His parents were of respectable middle-class stock; his father was Johannes Rubens, doctor-at-law, councillor and alderman of the city of Antwerp. The family had fled from Antwerp in 1566 in the face of the Spanish threat to the Low Countries, and beacuse the elder Rubens was suspected of Calvinist tendencies. They settled in Cologne in 1568, and here they met with further misfortunes. The elder Rubens involved himself in a clandestine love affair with Anne of Saxony, the second wife of William the Silent, Prince of Orange, the champion of the Protestant cause. The discovery of the affair led to his imprisonment and condemnation to death. From these distresses he was rescued by his wife, who appears to have been of stronger and more practical character than he. She obtained first the remission of the death sentence, then the release of her husband. The family were forced to leave Cologne and go to the little town of Siegen, and here Peter Paul Rubens was born.

The story of Rubens's childhood and early training is sketchily documented and soon enough told. After a certain interval the family got permission to return once more to Cologne, and there in March 1587 the elder Rubens died. The family then went back to Antwerp. At the age of fourteen Rubens began his apprenticeship to court-life by taking service as a page to Marguerite de Ligne-Arenberg, widow of a former governor of Antwerp.

This employment seems not to have lasted long, for soon Rubens began his apprenticeship as a painter in the studio of Tobias Verhaecht, who was a relation. From here he passed to the studio of Adam van Noort, and from there again to that of Otto van Veen. In 1598 Rubens was elected member of the Guild of St Luke—which meant, in effect, that he then graduated and was accepted as a fully fledged professional painter. Of these three masters, the one whose influence is most immediately traceable in Rubens's early work is Otto van Veen, a typical Flemish 'Romanist' of the period, cultivated but somewhat cold and uninspired. He had been court-painter first of all to Alessandro Farnese, who conquered the southern Netherlands for the Catholic cause, and later to the Regents, the Infanta Isabella, daughter of Philip II of Spain, and her husband the Archduke Albert, son of Emperor Maximilian II. It may have been van Veen, with these inclinations and sympathies, who implanted in Rubens the desire to study in Italy. And it was perhaps through van Veen's connection with the court that Rubens obtained a recommendation to Vicenzo Gonzaga, Duke of Mantua. At any rate, Rubens set out for Italy on May 9th, 1600, and was duly accepted into the Duke's service.

The Years in Italy

The little court of Mantua was a cultivated one. Vincenzo Gonzaga was interested not only in painting but in science and in music. He corresponded with Galileo and employed Monteverdi. Rubens was soon put to work. He made copies of other masters for the Duke; he painted his earliest altarpieces and allegorical and mythological pictures, and he scored a brilliant success as a portrait painter. This particular branch of painting was something of a specialty of Flemish artists in Italy at this time, as their Italian contemporaries considered portraits somewhat beneath them. Another northern partrait painter working at the Mantuan court was Frans Pourbus, and it is significant that Rubens's portraits of this period are difficult to distinguish from those of his less talented contemporary. Both of them painted in the internationally accepted court portrait style—smooth, cold, still held in the fetters of Mannerism. The great Baroque revolution was not yet fully under way.

Rubens was not confined to Mantua. He travelled extensively in Italy. After a period of residence in Rome, he was dispatched by the Duke of Mantua, in 1603, as member of an embassy to Spain. This was to be the first of many diplomatic missions undertaken by Rubens in the course of his life, and was followed by another period of residence in Rome, during which Rubens came into contact with the brilliantly original and tragically short-lived painter Adam Elsheimer, whose influence left some traces in his work.

In 1607 Rubens returned to the court of Mantua. In 1608 he received news of the serious illness of his mother and decided to hurry home to see her. He arrived too late—but he was never to return to Italy. The first phase of his career was over.

Rubens's Italian Style

Rubens's Italian period is still the least well-mapped of his career. He was at this period still discovering what he wanted to do and what he was capable of doing. He was looking, studying, being influenced. He was also undergoing, in his own person, the transition from Mannerist to Baroque.

The earliest works Rubens painted in Italy show a classicist Mannerism with borrowings from the Venetians—not so much Titian, whose full impact Rubens was not to feel until later, but Bassano and Veronese. He also, perhaps, felt some influence from the famous frescoes by Giulio Romano in the Palazza del Te, which was the summer residence of the court of Mantua. But it is impossible to trace here exactly all the various influences which Rubens sustained during his Italian visit. He seems to have had the happy talent of being able to assimilate what he required from any master who had something to teach him.

A special word, however, must be reserved for two important influences. The first was acquired during Rubens's first visit to the Spanish court, which gave him an opportunity to see the unrivalled Venetian pictures in the Spanish royal collections. It is oddly enough here, at the fountainhead of stiffness and etiquette, that Rubens begins to show the first traces of the liveliness of the Baroque in his work. The freedom of Titian and Tintoretto urged him towards a still greater freedom in his own work.

The other influence was that of the great revolutionary artist of the period in Italy Caravaggio (1573-1609). This influence persists through an important part of Rubens's career and is especially important in some of his most celebrated religious works. But it is still important to remember that Rubens also had the breadth of mind to be influenced by the very opposite school to that of Carravaggio—the school founded and led by Annibale Carracci, the Bolognese classicist. Where Caravaggio was a great individualist, who evolved his pictures actually on the canvas, Annibale was a thoroughly systematic painter. Rubens was deeply influenced by Carracci's methods. From him, he learned to work out the details of the composition beforehand, in innumerable sketches. In some of these, he studied the composition as a whole. In others, he worked out a single figure in more detail. Often he borrowed from the repertoire of motifs which Annibale had invented, especially those which he used for his greatest work, the ceiling of the gallery in the Palazzo Farnese. To Annibale's example we owe the splendid legacy of drawings which Rubens left behind him.

Rubens returned to Antwerp a more fully equipped and gifted painter than any other in Flanders. He was an immediate success. In 1609 he was appointed court painter to the Regents of the Netherlands, and in the same year he made his first marriage, to Isabella Brandt.

Rubens's life now settled into the pattern which it was to keep until his death, thirty-one years later. Almost the only differences were those brought by ever-increasing fame and ever-increasing prosperity. Rubens cut a figure not only in the world of art, but in the great world of affairs. He rapidly became a trusted adviser of the Infanta's, and she came to rely on him more and more after the death of her husband in 1621. Rubens undertook diplomatic missions—to Paris, to Spain, to England—and these in turn spread his fame and brought him new commissions. He took pride in displaying his learning and his universality. Contemporary accounts describe him as painting, conversing to visitors, being read to, and dictating a letter, all at the same time. We learn from his correspondence not only of his artistic and diplomatic concerns, but also of his interest in matters of scholarship and in his collections of objects of art. One of the most celebrated of ancient cameo-carvings, the 'Rubens Vase', bears that name because it once belonged to him.

Rubens's Methods of Work

Rubens's methods of work also took on the pattern which they were to keep for the rest of his career. These methods have been the subject of much later difficulty to art historians and connoisseurs. For Rubens was receiving much more in the way of commissions than one man could possibly handle alone, and—as was customary at that period—he adopted various expedients to fulfil them. The chief of these was the setting up of what amounted to a 'picture factory'. A celebrated letter of 1618 to Sir Dudley Carleton, the British ambassador at The Hague, gives us some insight into these methods. Rubens is offering an exchange of pictures for Carleton's collection of 'antiques', or works of Greek and Roman art, and he attaches a list of the pictures he is prepared to offer. Some of the entries in this list are very revealing:

'500 florins. A Prometheus chained on Mount Caucasus, with an eagle eating his liver. Original, by my own hand, the eagle painted by Snyders. 6 ×8 ft.

'600 florins. Leopards from life, with Satyrs and Nymphs. Original, by my hand, with the exception of a most beautiful landscape, by the hand of a master skilled in the genre. 9 ×11 ft.

'1,200 florins. A Last Judgement, begun by one of my pupils, after one I did in a much bigger size for the Most Serene Prince of Neurburg, who paid me three thousand five hudred florins cash for it; but this, as it is not finished, would be entirely retouched by my own hand, and will pass as an original.

'600 florins. A hunt of men on horseback and lions, begun by one of my pupils, after one which I painted for His Serenity of Bavaria, but all retouched by my hand.'

These four entries give us some notion of the different categories of picture which issued from Rubens's workshops. Besides those which he painted entirely himself, there were those which he painted with the assistance of specialist collaborators, mature artists such as Snyders and Jan Breughel, and those again which were painted with much or little intervention from pupils and members of the workshop. Finally, there were those productions which went out under the master's name but which he had never touched with his own hand. Very few of Rubens's large commissions—which include his most celebrated works—can be entirely without some contribution from other hands. In fact, most of the works which we can be quite sure are his alone are the oil-sketches in which Rubens worked out his first thoughts, decided on the plan of action, and laid down the lines which others were to follow.

Many of Rubens's collaborators were men of high talent. Perhaps the most celebrated of them were van Dyck and Jordaens, both of whom, in their later careers, developed different aspects of Rubens's art.

Pictures were not the only thing which issued from the Rubens shop. Rubens supplied designs for tapestries, designs for title pages, designs for decorative features at public events—every aspect of the visual arts came within his scope. Some of his letters show the painter taking particular care to secure the copyright in engravings after his works.

The Development of Rubens

Rubens's development as a painter is a smooth and continuous process without noticeable leaps forward and sudden breaks in style. The manner which Rubens brought back with him from Italy develops gradually into that of the so-called First Antwerp

Period—or rather into the two styles of this period. The Italian style of Rubens is hard but heroic. Violence of action is sometimes disconcertingly combined with coldness of technique. Of this style, the *Hero and Leander* (Plate I) is a typical example. When Rubens returns to Antwerp he gradually moves towards a method of painting which is more suave, but still solid. The famous picture at Munich, *Rubens with his first wife, Isabella Brandt* (Plate II) shows Rubens at the very beginning of this process. The painting is still comparatively tight, and traces of the style of portrait painting popular in Italy are still visible.

The two styles practised by Rubens in the First Antwerp Period are both of them more fluent and warmer. One manner is that of *The Descent from the Cross* in Antwerp Cathedral (the finished model for this is illustrated in Plate IV), and the *Christ's charge to Peter*, now in the Wallace Collection, London (Plate IX). Both these pictures are notable for the way in which Rubens keeps the figures and the action parallel to the picture-plane. There is no violent penetration of the picture-space, the design is balanced, solidly constructed, and the paint is smooth.

The other manner is much more distinctively Baroque. It is characterised by the energy, the continuous flow, which we associate with that style. The design for *The conversion of St Bavo* (Plate III), for example, shows a driving force which unites all the figures in one action, which draws the eye inwards with energetic diagonals and carefully linked forms. More Baroque still is the famous *Lion hunt* at Munich (Plate XI), though even here, for all its apparent wildness, the design is most carefully constructed and balanced.

The 1620's bring a reinforcement of this current in Rubens's work: the compositions of this period are marked by a characteristic restlessness, visible, for example, in *The death of Maxentius* (Plate XV). At the same time the brushwork begins to grow more fluid, and the palette, especially in the colours used for the flesh tones, becomes warmer.

This is the point in Rubens's development at which he more or less takes leave of his contemporaries. The painters of his own time could follow him thus far, and between the years 1609 and 1625, he formed the style of a whole generation of painters. After this point they can only follow him imperfectly, if at all.

The Later Works

The later works of Rubens, those subsequent to 1625, show the development of what is now regarded as his most personal and characteristic manner. This manner is marked by its fluidity, its extreme and unhesitating rapidity. The paint is usually quite thin, and the modelling is expressed by the free stroke of the brush.

This manner of painting had already been developed by Rubens in his oil sketches, made in preparation for larger works. Nothing, for instance, could be freer and livelier than the sketch for the *Lion hunt* now at Houghton Hall in Norfolk, yet this comes comparatively early in Rubens's development. Perhaps what gradually drew Rubens towards using this manner for his 'finished' paintings was the way in which work was undertaken in his studio. As far as we can discover, what happened was this: the pupils would lay in a picture either from Rubens's original sketch or from a composition already completed by the master, and the picture would, perhaps with a few corrections by Rubens, be taken to the point where it was almost completed. Rubens would then inspect the work, and would make such final corrections as he deemed fit with his own hand. This process involved, often, the pulling together of the work already done by rapid, unhesitating sweeps of the brush. This way of painting gradually became Rubens's practice even when he was not working over what others had done.

This new technique was accompanied by a reconciliation of Rubens's two previous manners of constructing a composition. His 'classical' manner fuses with his 'Baroque' one to create a way of painting which is at once warmer than the former and more balanced than the latter. A good example of this way of painting is *The rape of the Sabines* (Plate XXXVII). Here, though the action is energetic and violent enough, the composition is very carefully balanced; each stress, each diagonal, has an opposing stress or diagonal designed to keep the picture in equilibrium. The forces at work in the picture are strong, but they are completely contained within the rectangle of the frame.

It is interesting to remember that Rubens's latest manner has certain affinities with Abstract Impressionism. Rubens, too, trusts himself to the nature of the medium itself, its fluidity, its mobility. He, too, governs the structure of the picture by the movement of the brush; the stroke itself is the most important element in building up the lines of force. But these techniques are not pursued as ends in themselves—they are brought into relationship with the world of natural appearances, and it is the conflict and reconciliation between the way of painting and the way of seeing which gives these late works something of their fascination.

Realism and Idealism in Rubens

Perhaps this is the appropriate point at which to say something about Rubens's relationship to the concept of 'realism' in painting. He occupies, in fact, rather a curious position, and one which has never been satisfactorily defined. He is not, it seems obvious, an 'idealising' artist in the sense in which we usually understand that word. One of the most frequent complaints lodged against him by critics is that, though the compositions are noble, their effect is often diminished by the personages who form the separate units in the composition. When we think of the types Rubens habitually uses for, say, the Madonna, or for St Joseph, they seem too close to same actual, living model, and it is difficult to deny that Rubens fails to give them that universality which we find in the sixteenth-century Italian painters. And this is the root cause of the criticisms levelled against Rubens's paintings of nudes, especially the female nudes. These bodies are too much particular bodies, the expression of an individual taste and an individual and powerful sensuality. They do not speak to us as an expression of our common humanity; they are too closely characterised for that. And this can make us squeamish. It is not their forms that move us, nor even the sweep of their outlines, but something more material—their pearly textures, their very 'fleshiness'. Of all the artists who ever painted flesh, Rubens—especially the Rubens of after 1625—is the most successful in making us realise its beauty of colour and texture. He gives it a translucency, an inner glow, which not even Renoir could achieve.

But granted that Rubens cannot be counted as an idealist—we cannot call him especially 'realistic' either. His figures certainly do not strike us as straightforward transcriptions of reality. One only has to think of some of the Dutch seventeenth-century masters to realise how far Rubens is from them. In Rubens everything is larger than life; both men and women spring from some energetic race of giants. Their anatomies have been recreated; they conform to a canon which is pictorial rather than natural. Flesh, bone and sinew have been entirely re-cast; muscles swell where none are to be seen in nature. These beings bear the same relation to the ordinary physical appearance of ordinary humans as the heightened language of the orator bears to the language of conversation.

Rubens ignores both the ideal and the real because he is fundamentally uninterested in either. He is interested, instead, in the expression of energy and appetite. We enter into his pictures because he heightens our perceptions of gesture and movement; he makes us experience rhythm rather as music does. He does not attempt to diminish our attachment to purely physical sensations; instead he makes us experience them more intensely, and in a new way.

Rubens as a Religious Painter

Rubens's work divides, from the point of view of subject matter, into several categories. Of these, the religious paintings are perhaps the least discussed today. Since among these works with religious themes are some of those for which Rubens was most famous and most praised both in this own times and in the eighteenth and even the nineteenth century it is worthwhile taking a look at the attitudes which they express.

At first, their lack of reticence may offend us. The emotions are all there on the surface; we participate willy-nilly, merely by looking. When pictures of martyrdoms, or of the events of the Passion, are in question, this can seem somewhat 'shocking'. But these are not pictures which set out to shock, as do those of similar subjects by Caravaggio. They are the expression of a place and a time as much as of the artist's own religious attitudes. Rubens, for all his father's Calvinist leanings, seems to have been a man of genuine and orthodox Catholic views. In his religious pictures he paints in a way which was throughly acceptable both to his patrons and his fellow citizens—so much so that his initial success when he returned to Antwerp was based on these commissions.

Flemish Catholicism was a popular religion in which all members of the community participated. Popular fervour was general and genuine. Rubens's canvases are essentially popular and public statements. They are given added force by a number of other factors. The first is that Catholicism was to some extent more embattled and militant in Flanders than it was elsewhere, and had been so ever since religious differences began to rend apart the northern and the southern halves of the Netherlands in the sixteenth century. The second factor is the nature of Baroque art itself. This style, of which Rubens was one of the leading exponents, came into being partly through the demands made on the visual arts by religion. Like all the arts, painting had been pressed into the service of the Counter-Reformation, and the devices which we think of as characteristically Baroque in architecture, sculpture and painting are just those which make the spectator no longer spectator but participant in some religious event, whether painted on canvas, carved out of marble, or taking place within some building designed for the purpose.

There was, in any case, a strong tradition of religious painting of this popular kind in Flanders, which had been established by the van Eycks and their immediate successors. This tradition Rubens still clings to. Though the style is totally different, his attitudes and those of the Flemish Primitives are not wholly dissimilar. A Deposition by Rogier van der Weyden has a deliberately accentuated pathos, which we find again in Rubens. Even the most disagreeably bloody of Rubens's martyrdoms can be paralleled only too easily among his Primitive predecessors.

Rubens as an Allegorist

One aspect of Rubens's art which was much appreciated by his contemporaries is now almost wasted upon most of his audience. The most spectacular examples of his powers in this direction are the two great decorative cycles, the *History of Marie de Médicis* (See Plates XVIII–XXI) and the *Whitehall Ceiling* (See Plates XXVII–XXX). Here a profusion of mythological and symbolic personages and attributes are deployed across the huge canvases. Today we appreciate them for the sweep and vigour of the compositions, the energy expressed by the actions and gestures of the personages. But Rubens's contemporaries read them closely for their political meanings, and Rubens's patrons considered this political meaning almost the most important aspect of the work.

Marie de Médicis and her court put Rubens to endless trouble before the programme for the series of paintings for the Luxembourg was approved, and completion was somewhat delayed because of the changes imposed on the work. The whole episode illustrates both the advantages and the disadvantages of the system of patronage which then formed the economic basis of the artist's existence. Patrons considered themselves free to lay down a programme of subjects for the artist. It was up to him to use his skill and imagination to turn into visual terms what the patron wished expressed. Oddly enough, though quarrels between artists and patrons inevitably occurred, artists never seem to have felt that this particular yoke was too heavy to be borne. And the close, if sometime overdemanding, interest of princely patrons in the visual arts all over Europe produced the steady flow of commissions on which Rubens depended for his magnificent scale of living.

It is perhaps worthwhile, too, to remark on the way in which Rubens's use of allegory differed from that of the painters of the Italian Renaissance. If one compares, say, *Henry IV receiving the portrait of Marie de Médicis* (Plate XVIII) with Botticelli's *Primavera* from the point of view of the symbolism employed, one sees that Rubens is much more simple and direct in his methods. His mythological personages have perfectly straightforward parts to play in the exaltation of his patrons' beauty and virtute. In Botticelli the symbolism is involved, complex, esoteric—so much so that the *Primavera* continues to provoke a good deal of scholarly controversy. The attitudes of the two artists towards the use of allegorical devices are in fact very different. Botticelli is displaying his learning, he is painting as a scholar for the appreciation of other scholars. His symbolism is intentionally difficult. This is far from being the case with Rubens. His allegories are meant to be understood easily by any man who could call himself educated. He appeals very largely to that knowledge of the classics which formed the basis of the educational system of the time. If we now miss the points he is trying to make, it is not through the artists's deliberately contrived obscurity, but because common knowledge—the stock of things all educated men are expected to know—has altered.

Rubens as a Portraitist

It now remains to say something about Rubens's contributions to the two branches of painting which are most easily understood by his present-day audience. In one of them he has commonly roused less enthusiasm than in the other. Rubens's portraits have sometimes been criticised for the lack of true 'character'. It has been said that, since he was an artist who did not submit himself easily or completely to the discipline of visual appearances, so his portraits contain too much of his own personality and too little of that of the sitter. It is true that he endows those whom he painted with something of his own air of radiant energy and vitality. A glance at the portrait, *Thomas, Earl of Arundel*

(Plate xxv) is sufficient to prove this. But still the sitter remains himself; he lives on the canvas in a way that a more meticulous and plodding painter could hardly manage to make him. But one thing must be admitted, and that is that Rubens's portraits do not achieve the mysterious and touching poetry, the ineffable distinction and aristocracy, we find in some portraits by van Dyck, especially those of van Dyck's English period.

In portraying his own family, however, Rubens achieved an intimacy, an easy tenderness which we hardly find again until we come to some of the portraits painted by the Impressionists. The affinity between Rubens's depictions of his second wife, Hélène Fourment, and some of Renoir's most delightful works is very striking. But these paintings by Rubens are hardly portraits in the true sense at all. They are not attempts to seize the very essence of a character but expressions of the artists's most intimate feelings, a mixture of sensuality and tenderness.

Rubens as a Landscape Painter

Few, if any, voices have ever been raised against Rubens's achievement as a landscape painter. Even those who profess no great liking for his work make an exception for the landscapes. And of all Rubens's works these are certainly the most brilliantly original. He is the first to paint landscape in terms of atmosphere, the first to concentrate on conveying with the utmost freshness and immediacy his own reactions to a particular place, a particular kind of light, a particular condition of atmosphere. And the freedom and directness of the technique he adopted was to have a liberating effect on subsequent landscape painting.

Many of the landscapes are of the countryside near his own castle of Steen, near Malines, which he bought in 1635 (see–Plates xxxlx–xli). And he approaches this evidently very much loved countryside in much the same way in which he set out to paint Hélène Fourment. His pictures are examinations and explanations of his own state of feeling rather than literal transcriptions of reality.

Rubens's Influence

Rubens, of almost all the painters who ever lived, has exercised the most direct and fruitful influence on his successors. Not only were there two very important masters among his immediate following, in the persons of Anthony van Dyck and Jacob Jordaens and not only did he exercise the strongest influence on many artists of his own time, but this influence continued well into the two succeeding centuries. Curiously enough, it proved most fruitful outside Flanders. The whole course of French painting in the eighteenth century and the first half of the nineteenth consists in the history of Rubens's influence. It was Rubens who provided Watteau with both the technical means and the inspiration to break away from the dead classicism of the age of Louis XIV. Fragonard and Boucher equally show the dominating influence of Rubens. And after the classical reaction initiated and led by David, Delacroix once more returns to Rubens for his inspiration. In England, Rubens's influence is less clearly characterised but just as persistent. Something of him is to be found in most of the English eighteenth-century portraitists. Reynolds attempts to reinterpret some of his effects. And minor figures, such as James Ward, are completely dominated and overwhelmed by his genius.

Rubens is an artist who arouses strong feelings of attraction and repulsion, rather than an artist who, like Poussin, invite our considered admiration. He has roused many men, and particularly artists, to make brilliant comments on his work, and a selection from these will be found in this book. But when we come to the final verdict it is hard not to fall back on the simple comment of Eugène Fromentin, who was both artist and critic at once. This is what he says: 'Do we admire? Not always. Can we remain unmoved? Scarcely ever.'

Outline Biography of Rubens

1577	June 28th. Peter Paul Rubens born at Siegen in Westphalia.
1587	His father dies in Cologne, and soon after the family move to Antwerp.
1590	Becomes a page in the service of Marguerite de Ligne-Arenberg, widow of a former governor of Antwerp.
1592–96	Works in the studio of the painter Adam van Noort.
1596	For four years, works with Otto van Veen, court-painter to Archduke Albrecht.
1598	Elected a member of the Guild of St Luke and accepted as a fully fledged professional painter.
1600	Obtains a recommendation to Vicenzo Gonzaga, Duke of Mantua, and sets out for Italy on May 9th. Enters the service of Gonzaga in Mantua.
1600–02	Takes up residence in Rome.
1603	Pays his first visit to Spain as a member of an embassy from the Duke of Mantua.
1605–07	Is again in residence in Rome where he meets the painter Adam Elsheimer. Returns to Mantua in 1607.
1608	Receives news of his mother's ill-health and returns to Antwerp to find that she is no longer alive.

1609	Is appointed court-painter to the Regents of the Netherlands on September 23rd. A moth later he marries Isabella Brandt.
1613	Paints *The Descent from the Cross* for Antwerp Cathedral.
1615–16	Van Dyck enters his workshop.
1620	He paints *Le Coup de Lance* and the decorations for the church of St Charles Borromaeus in Antwerp.
1621–22	Makes the designs for the tapestries in the *Constantine Cycle*.
1622–25	Paints the *History of Marie de Médicis*, commissioned by the queen for the great gallery of the Luxembourg Palace.
1626	Isabella Brandt dies.
1628	He pays his second visit to Spain, again on a diplomatic mission. He is appointed secretary to the Netherlands Privy Council and is raised to the nobility.
1629–30	Visits London on diplomatic business and is knighted by Charles I. He receives the commission for the *Whitehall Ceiling*. In December of 1630, after four years a widower, he marries sixteen-year-old Hélène Fourment.
1629–34	At work on the *Whitehall Ceiling*, the canvases for which are finished on August 1st, 1634.
1635	He buys the Château de Steen and paints some of his finest landscape pictures.
1638	His health begins to fail.
1640	On May 27th, he makes his will, and on May 30th, he dies and is buried the same evening in the family vault in the church of St Jacques at Antwerp.

Some Comments on Rubens

The comments printed in this section were made by men who expressed themselves on the subject of Rubens from the standpoint of their own times, and without the aids to appreciation offered by modern scholarship. Neverthless, they possessed the enormous advantage of being practising artists. They knew what they wanted to do in their profession, and they judged Rubens from this standpoint, with reactions of admiration and envy.

Antoine Watteau (from a letter to Watteau's patron Julienne with reference to a painting by Rubens which had recently been given to the artist).

From the moment I received it, I have not had a moment's repose, and my eyes are never weary of returning towards the easel where I have placed it as if in a shrine.

Sir Joshua Reynolds (this carefully pondered verdict comes from Reynolds's *Journey to Flanders and Holland*).

The production of Rubens... seem to flow with a freedom and prodigality, as if they cost him nothing; and to the general animation of the composition there is always a correspondent spirit in the execution of the work. The striking brilliancy of his colour, and their lively opposition to each other, the flowing liberty and freedom of his outline, the animated pencil, with which every subject is touched, all contribute to awaken and keep alive the attention of the spectator; awaken in him, in some measure, correspondent sensations, and make him feel a degree of that enthusiasm with which the painter was carried away. To this we may add the complete uniformity in all parts of the work, so that the whole seems to be conducted, and grow out of one mind: everything is of a piece and fits its place. Even his taste of drawing and of form appears to correspond better with his colouring and composition than if he had adopted any other manner, though that manner, simply considered, might be better: it is here as in personal attractions; there is frequently found a certain agreement and correspondence in the whole together, which is often more captivating than more regular beauty.

Rubens appears to have had that confidence in himself, which it is necessary for every artist to assume, when he has finished his studies, and may venture in some measure to throw aside the fetters of authority, to consider the rules as subject to his control, and not himself subject to the rules; to risk and dare extraordinary attempts without a guide, abandoning himself to his own sensations depending upon them. To this confidence must be attributed the originality of manner by which he may be truly said to have extended the limits of the art. After Rubens had made up his manner, he never looked out of himself for assistance: there is consequently very little in his works that appears to be taken from other masters. If he has borrowed anything, he has had the address to change and adapt it so well to the rest of his work that the theft is not discoverable.

Beside the excellency of Rubens in these general powers, he possessed the true art of imitating. He saw the objects of nature with a painter's eye; he saw at once the predominant feature by which every object is known and distinguished: and as soon as seen, it was executed with a facility that is astonishing; and, let me add, this facility, is to a painter, when he closely examines a picture, a source of great pleasure. How far this excellence may be perceived or felt by those who are not painters, I know not: to them certainly it is not enough that objects be truly represented; they must likewise be represented with grace; which means here, that the work is done with facility nad without effort. Rubens was, perhaps, the greatest master in the mechanical part of the art, and the best workman with his tools, that ever exercised a pencil.

This part of the art, though it does not hold rank with the powers of invention, of giving character and expression, has yet in it what may be called genius. It is certainly something that cannot be taught by words, though it may be learned by a frequent examination of those pictures which possess this excellence. It is felt by very few Painters; and it is as rare at this time among the living Painters as any of the higher excellencies of the art.

This power, which Rubens possessed in the highest degree, enabled him to represent whatever he understood better than any other painter. His animals, particularly lions and horses, are so admirable, that it might be said they were never properly represented but by him. His portraits rank with the best works of the Painters who have made that branch of the art the sole business of their lives; and of these he has left a great variety of specimens. The same may be said for his landscapes: and though Claude Lorraine finished more minutely, as becomes a Professor in any particular branch, yet there is such an airiness and facility in the landscapes of Rubens, that a painter would as soon wish to be the author of them, as those of Claude, or any other artists whatever.

The pictures of Rubens have this effect on the spectator, that he finds himself in no wise disposed to pick out and dwell on his defects. The criticisms which are made on him are often unreasonable. His style ought no more to be blamed for not having the sublimity of Michael Angelo, than Ovid should be censured because he is not like Virgil.

However, it must be acknowledged that he wanted many excellencies, which would have perfectly united with his style. Among those we may reckon beauty in his female characters: sometimes indeed they make approaches to it; they are healthy comely women, but seldom, if ever possess any degree of excellence. The same may be said for his young men and children: his old men have that sort of dignity which a bushy beard will confer; but he never possessed a poetical conception of character. In his representation of the highest characters in the Christian or the fabulous world, instead of something above humanity, which might fill the idea which is concevied of such beings, the spectator finds little more than mere mortals, such as he meets with every day...

The difference of the manner of Rubens, from that of any other painter before him, is in nothing more distinguishable, than in his colouring, which is totally different from that of Titian, Correggio, or any of the great colourists. The effect of his pictures may be not improperly compared to clusters of flowers; all his colours appear as clear and beautiful; at the same time he has avoided the tawdry effect which one would expect such gay colours to produce: in this respect resembling Barocci more than any other painter. What was said of an ancient painter, may be applied to those two artists,—that their figures look as if they fed upon roses...

To conclude: I will venture to repeat in favour of Rubens what I have before said in regard to the Dutch School—that those who cannot see the extraordinary merit of this great painter, either have a narrow conception of the variety of art, or are led away by the affectation of approving nothing but what comes from the Italian School.

Eugène Delacroix (all his life Delacroix remained fascinated by Rubens, and no other painter is mentioned so often in his famous *Journal*).

April 30th, 1847
With all the outspokenness of his colours and his heavy forms, he arrives at an ideal of the greatest power. Force, vehemence and splendour free him from the demands of grace and charm.

Loose leaf in the Journal for 1847

Rubens arrives, having already forgotten the traditions of grace and of simplicity. Through his genius he recreates an ideal. We get strength, striking effects, and expression pushed to its limit.

June 8th, 1850

How many magnificent compositions would be nothing without the great cook's grain of salt! That power of the *indefinable something* is astonishing with Rubens; what his temperament, his *vis poetica*, adds to a composition, without seeming to change it, is prodigious.

October 12th, 1853

Rubens is a remarkable example of the abuse of details. His painting, in which imagination dominates, is everywhere superabundant; his accessories are too much worked out; his picture is like a meeting where they all speak at once. And yet, if you compare that exuberant manner—I will not say to the dryness and poverty of modern work—but to very beautiful pictures where nature has been imitated with sobriety and a greater regard for truth, you will soon feel that the true painter is the one in whom imagination speaks before all else.

October 27th, 1860

That man Rubens is admirable. What a magician! I get out of sorts with him at times. I quarrel with him because of his heavy forms, his lack of science and elegance. But how far he is above all those little qualities which make up the whole baggage of others. Here is a man, anyway, who has the courage to be himself: he forces one to accept those so-called defects which come from that force which sweeps along the man himself: they subjugate us in spite of the precepts which stand good for everyone in the world—except him...

Rubens does not chasten himself, and he is right. By allowing himself everything he carries one beyond the limit scarcely attained by the most eminent painters; he dominates one, he overpowers one, with all his liberty and boldness.

Rubens's Philosophy of Art

The nearest Rubens ever came to making a formal statement of his artistic aims is the letter printed here. It was addressed to Franciscus Junius, a Dutch scholar who was at this period the Earl of Arundel's librarian. Junius had just sent Rubens a copy of his book *De Pictura Veterum* (*on the Painting of the Ancients*) and this is Rubens's letter of thanks. The original is partly in Flemish, partly in Latin.

August 1st, 1637

Sir,

You will certainly have been surprised not to get news, after so long, of the arrival of your book, which as your kind letter of May 24th proves, was sent me on that date. I beg you, however, to believe that your book was not given to me until a fortnight ago by one Leon Hemelsroy, with many excuses for being so late with it. And here is the reason why I did not reply sooner to your letter, for I wished first of all to see and read the book, and I have now done so attentively. In truth, I find that you have done our art much honour by this immense treasury, which you have excavated from antiquity with so much care, and arranged in such an orderly fashion. In a word, your book is truly a rich storehouse of all the examples, rules and regulations proper to our art and scattered everywhere in the writings of the ancients, and preserved till our own day to our great profit. I believe, then, that you have fully justified your title *De Pictura Veterum*, and that you have achieved your aim of citing the opinions, the laws, the judgements and the examples which illuminate the question for us, of reproducing them with an admirable erudition and in a most elegant style, of putting your work in the best order, and of giving it the highest finish even in the least details. But now that we can, each according to his fancy and his talent, model ourselves upon the ancient painters, I wish that an equally accomplished work would be devoted to the Italian painters, who have left us examples and models, which today can still be seen by everyone and which can, so to speak, be pointed to and explained in the original.

For that which is perceived through the senses produces a greater and more durable impression, demands more profound examination and provides richer material for study than that which we see only in our imaginations and as if dreaming, or else obscured by words which we try three times to seize (as Orpheus tried to seize Eurydice) and which slip away from us and deceive our hopes. We speak of this from experience, for how few of us who wish to represent in reality some masterpiece by Apelles or Thimantes described by Pliny or by other writers find something sufficiently ingenious and conforming to the majesty of Ancient Art. But a man obedient only to his own taste will drink as a great vintage some nondescript wine, and will offend the souls of those great artists whom I venerate profoundly and whose traces, I admit, I worship rather than imagining that I am able to equal them, except in thought. I beg you, Sir, to forgive me all that I say here in the freedom of friendship, in the hope that having served us the first course you will not refuse us the main dish which we desire so eagerly. Until now, all those who have dealt with the matter have not satisfied our appetite, for artistic individualities must be spoken of as I have said. With this, I recommend myself with all my heart to your good graces and thank you greatly for the honour and the friendship which you have shown me in giving your book to me, remaining as ever, Sir,

Your humble and affectionate servant,

PETER PAUL RUBENS

Notes on the Plates

Plate I   *Hero and Leander*, c. 1606. Oil on canvas. 36³/₄ ×50¹/₄ in. (92.5 × 126.5 cm.). New Haven, Conn., Yale University Art Gallery.

This fine picture is a characteristic example of Rubens's exuberant style during his visit to Italy. It was probably painted in Rome or in Genoa about 1606. It seems to have been in the collection of the Duke of Buckingham, and it certainly belonged later on to Charles II's court painter, Sir Peter Lely. There is a later and larger version of the composition in the Dresden Gemäldegalerie.

With its stormy violence and high-pitched excitement, *Hero and Leander* anticipates some of the best-known compositions of the Romantic painters of the nineteenth century. In particular it makes a very interesting comparison with the *Raft of the Medusa* by Géricault, in the Louvre.

Plate II   *Rubens with his first wife, Isabella Brandt*, c. 1609. Oil on canvas. 69 ×52¹/₄ in. (174 ×132 cm.). Munich, Bayerische Staatsgemäldesammlungen.

This picture seems to have been designed as a 'wedding portrait', and therefore will have been painted immediately after Rubens's return from Italy. In style it makes a very interesting contrast with the much later 'family' portraits of Hélène Fourment and her children. Here the handling is much stiffer and tighter, much closer, in fact, to the international Mannerist portrait style which Rubens had practised at the court of Mantua. This effect of rigidity is reinforced by the less flowing style of dress fashionable at this time, when compared with that adopted later in the seventeenth century.

The physical resemblance between Isabella Brandt and Hélène Fourment has often been remarked by commentators; also the likeness which both of them bear to the female type which Rubens adopted in much of his painting. Fromentin comments, in *Les Maîtres d'Autrefois*: 'From the first years of Rubens's life a certain ineffable form seems to have taken possession of his heart, an unchangeable ideal haunted his amorous and constant imagination. He takes delight in it, he completes it, he achieves it. He pursued it, in a way, in both his marriages, just as he never stopped repeating in it his works. There is always something of both Isabella and Hélène in every woman he modelled upon one of them. In the first he seems to put a preconceived trait of the second; in the second he inserts a vague but indelible memory of the first.'

Plate III

The conversion of St Bavo, c. 1612. Oil on panel. 43 ×64³/₄ in. (109 ×165 cm.). London, National Gallery.

This is the sketch for the altarpiece in the church of St Bavo, Ghent. St Bavo is the patron saint of the dioceses of Ghent and Haarlem. He is traditionally supposed to have been a nobleman named Count Allowin, who lived from 589 to 654, and who in his early years led a very wild and dissolute life. He was converted by St Amandus (who is here seen receiving him into the life of religion). Later St Bavo founded a monastery on his lands at Ghent, and from this the present church of St Bavo takes its origin.

Rubens creates an impressive feeling of drama merely by the way in which he groups his figures; a strong rhythm informs the whole composition and draws our eyes to the central figure. Beneath the main scene is a secondary one of alms-giving, which contrasts with the noble ceremony above—misery is played off against splendour. The whole is an impressive example of the way in which a great Baroque composer can be dramatic without the necessity to resort to violent action.

Plate IV

The Descent from the Cross, c. 1613. Oil on panel. 45 ×30 in. (113.5 ×75.5 cm.). London, Courtauld Institute of Art.

This is a large, finished model, perhaps made for the client's approval, for the centre section of the famous altarpiece in Antwerp Cathedral. It is, perhaps, a little fresher and freer than the finished work, and has been endowed with more pathos.

The composition, which is mostly in one plane to the picture-surface, represents the 'classicising' aspect of Rubens's art during the First Antwerp Period. It also shows strong traces of the influence of Caravaggio.

Impressive and moving as this picture is, Fromentin's verdict on the completed altarpiece is probably a just one. He says: 'The scene is powerful and grave. Its effect is visible at a distance. It is most impressive on the wall; it is serious and it makes one feel serious too. When we think of the murders which cover Rubens's works with blood, the massacres, the executioners who torture, who tear the flesh and raise shrieks of agony, we see that this is a noble piece of torment. Everything is restrained, concise, laconic, as if it were a page of Holy Scripture... Rubens recollects himself, watches himself, restrains himself, is completely master of his powers, keeps them in hand, only makes use of half of them.'

Plate V

Studies of the head of a Negro, c. 1614. Oil on canvas. 18½ ×24¹/₄ in. (47 ×61 cm.). Brussels, Royal Museum of Fine Arts.

Solidly constructed, yet completely spontaneous, these sketches show Rubens's special talent for creating types. In particular, he seems to have been interested in, and excited by, the less familiar appearance of the Negro, as these are often painted with special brilliance where they appear in his pictures.

Plate VI   *Nature adorned by the Graces*, 1613–15. Oil on panel. 42 ×28½ in. (106.7 ×72.4 cm.). Glasgow, art Gallery and Museum.

This picture, which probably once belonged to Charles I's favourite, the Duke of Buckingham, is one of the most important extant examples of the collaboration between Rubens and Jan Breughel de Velours. While the bulk of the work is from Rubens's own hand, Breughel painted the swag of fruit and flowers.

Rubens shows his classical erudition in this picture by representing nature in the guise of a term of the many-breasted Diana of the Ephesians.

Plate VII   *The Holy Family*, c. 1615. Oil on panel. 50 ×36¼ in. (127 ×91.7 cm.). London, Wallace Collection.

This picture seems to have been painted for the oratory of Archduke Albert, Rubens's patron and Regent of the Netherlands. Afterwards it was in the Imperial Gallery in Vienna, but was given away by Emperor Joseph II as a reward for services rendered.

The effect of the light on the Virgin's face is very like that in *Le Chapeau de Paille* (Plate XVII)

Plate VIII   *The union of Earth and Water*, c. 1615. Oil on panel. 13¾ ×12 in. (35 ×30.5 cm.). Cambridge, Fitzwilliam Museum.

The very high quality of this sketch has been newly revealed by recent cleaning. Rubens's sketches are among the most attractive part of his work—utterly spontaneous, wonderfully responsive to the qualities of the medium, they appeal especially to modern taste. The female nude here is interesting as illustrating the difference between the conceptions of Rubens and Jordaens. Where Jordaens would have looked for a fully plastic effect, Rubens models surprisingly lightly, through the direction of the brushstroke more than anything else.

The picture for which this is a sketch is now in the Hermitage Museum, Leningrad.

Plate IX   *Christ's charge to Peter*, c. 1616. Oil on panel. 54 ×46½ in. (136 ×117 cm.). London, Wallace Collection.

An altarpiece commissioned by one Nicolas Damant for the Chapel of the Holy Sacrament of the Church of St Gudule, Brussels. The Christ and the three apostles seem to be painted from the same models as those who appear in the *Incredulity of St Thomas* in Antwerp Museum. The heads of the two sheep in the bottom right-hand corner are intended as a reference to Christ's words to Peter: 'Feed my sheep!' For this reason the picture is sometimes known under the title *Ove Pasces*.

This kind of picture by Rubens—half-length figures treated in a rather coldly classical way—has not been universally admired. Sir Joshua Reynolds saw this picture when it was still in Flanders and said of it: 'The characters are heavy, without grace or dignity; the handling on close examination appears tame even to the suspicion of its being a copy;

the colouring is remarkably fresh. The name of Rubens would not stand high in the world, if he had never produced other pictures than such as this!'

Plate X   *Two satyrs*, c. 1615–17. Oil on panel. 30 ×26 in. (76 ×66 cm.). Munich, Bayerische Staatsgemäldesammlungen.

Rubens was fond of painting Dionysiac subjects, many of which are apt to seem a little coarse and over-boisterous to modern taste. This little picture is, however, a fine and subtle evocation of the Dionysiac atmosphere.

Plate XI   *Lion hunt*, 1617–18. Oil on canvas. 98 ×148³/₄ in. (247 ×375 cm.). Munich. Bayerische Staatsgemäldesammlungen.

This very celebrated picture is known to have been completed before April 28th, 1618. It was painted for Maximilian, Duke of Bavaria. Delacroix has some very interesting comments to make on the composition in his *Journal*: 'The rearing horses, the bristling manes, a thousand accessories, shields wrenched from the arms, bridles tangled — everything combines to strike the admiration, and the execution is admirable. But the picture has something confused about it, the eye does not know where to stop, it gets the feeling of a frightful disorder, and it seems that art has not presided sufficiently to increase, by prudent balance or by omission, the effect of so many inventions of genius.'

Though Delacroix was one of Rubens's most enthusiastic and sympathetic interpreters this comment seems curiously wrong-headed. It is true that the picture is in Rubens's most violently Baroque manner, but how admirably he has organised the abounding energy of his conception. It is particularly worth noting how the straight diagonal lines of the spears serve to bind the composition together.

Plate XII   *Christ in the tomb*, 1617–18. Oil on panel. 55 ×35³/₄ in. (139 ×90 cm.). Antwerp, Museum of Fine Arts.

Painted to adorn the tomb of Jan Michielsen, an Antwerp merchant, perhaps with the assistance of van Dyck. It illustrates the extreme pathos which Rubens could achieve in some of his religious compositions of this period.

Plate XIII   *Le Coup de Lance*, 1620. Oil on panel. 168½ ×123 in. (424 ×310 cm.). Antwerp, Museum of Fine Arts.

Commissioned by the Burgomaster Nicolas Rockox for the high altar of the Church of the Recollects at Antwerp, and the most famous of all Rubens's religious compositions, it seems to show the influence of the Venetian painters who had so much interested Rubens in Italy. The three crosses set on the diagonal occur previously in Tintoretto.

The figure of the Magdalen at the foot of the Cross has always been particularly admired. Jakob Burckhardt, the father of modern criticism of Rubens, comments on 'the art of interrupting some great story in the middle by a beautiful female figure',

30

and Reynolds says: 'This is by far the most beautiful profile I ever saw of Rubens, or, I think, of any other painter; the excellence of its colouring is beyond expression.'

Plate XIV *Adam and Eve driven out of Paradise*, 1620. Oil on panel 19½ ×25½ in. (49.5 ×64.5 cm.) Prague, National Gallery.

This is a sketch for part of the decoration in the Church of St Charles Borromaeus, Antwerp. The contract was signed on March 29th, 1620. Rubens agreed to deliver, by the end of the year, thirty-nine pictures for the aisles and gallery of the church. He agreed to execute all the sketches himself, but was allowed to use collaborators in making the finished pictures. The entire decoration was destroyed by fire on July 18th, 1718.

The treatment of trees and foliage in this sketch shows the tremendous freedom Rubens permitted himself in making these preparatory studies.

Plate XV *The death of Maxentius*, 1621–22. Oil on panel. 16½ ×26¾ in. (42 ×67.5 cm.). London, Wallace Collection.

Design for one of the twelve tapestries in the *Constantine Cycle*, commissioned from Rubens by Louis XIII of France. A complete series of these tapestries still exists in the Garde-Meuble in Paris. Rubens despatched the first four sketches in the series to the tapestry weaver in November 1622.

The sketch shows Rubens's interpretation of what was perhaps the most crucial event in the career of Emperor Constantine—his defeat, in 312, of the army of his rival Maxentius at Saxa Rubra near Rome. Maxentius and his army attempted to make their way back into the safety of the city via the Milvian Bridge, but the crowds forced the defeated emperor into the river where he was drowned, leaving Constantine master of Rome. Rubens uses these events as an excuse for painting an energetic Baroque battlepiece, in melting, pale colours.

Plate XVI *The Adoration of the Magi*, 1624. Oil on panel. 24⅞ ×18⅝ in. (63 ×47 cm.). London, Wallace Collection.

This is the model for the picture now in the Museum of Fine Arts, Antwerp, which was commissioned from Rubens in 1624 for the high altar of the Abbey of St Michel at Antwerp.

Rubens changed the composition considerably when he came to paint the finished picture. For example, the king who faces the spectator is turned into a Negro. An Antwerp merchant called Nicolas Respani seems to have been the model for this particular figure. In 1647 Respani left his portrait 'in Turkish costume, painted by Rubens' to his wife. The picture still exists at the Cassel Gallery and shows a strong resemblance to the figure as it appears here.

Plate XVII *Le Chapeau de Paille*, c. 1620–25. Oil on panel. 31 ×21½ in. (79 ×55 cm.). London, National Gallery.

This, one of the most beautiful of Rubens's portraits of women, is supposed to represent

Susanne Fourment, the third daughter of Daniel Fourment, and sister of Hélène Fourment. It is a mystery how it acquired its traditional title 'The Straw Hat', as the hat in question is obviously made of beaver. The effect of light in the face has often been admired, and many subsequent portraitist have tried to repeat it. Reynolds achieves something like it in his portrait, *Nelly O'Brien*, now in the Wallace Collection, London.

Plates XVIII-XXI

THE HISTORY OF MARIE DE MEDICIS

Marie de Médicis (1573–1642) was the second Medici queen of France. Henry IV married her as his second wife, and after his assassination she acted as regent for their young son Louis XIII. The immense series of pictures now in the Louvre which commemorate some of the phases of her somewhat stormy career were commissioned by her from Rubens for the great gallery of the Luxembourg Palace, construction of which was completed in 1620.

The project is first mentioned in a letter of December 23rd, 1621. Rubens then came to Paris to discuss the matter. He was resident there in January and February 1622. On May 19th, 1622 he submitted a general programme for the series, and the queen accepted this, but insisted on certain changes. By the end of May 1623, Rubens had brought nine pictures of the series with him to Paris, and to these he added the finishing touches after they had been put into position. The rest of the pictures were delivered in February 1625 and the gallery was finally inaugurated in the following May. Throughout the work Rubens was in continual consultation with the French court about the allegorical programme, and they compelled him to make many changes to meet their wishes.

The series is perhaps the most important single part of Rubens's entire enormous *oeuvre*, and nothing could better display his tireless invention and energy. Though the pictures are not entirely autograph, they are mostly of very high quality, and Rubens evidently took much trouble with them. It was perhaps the technique demanded of him here, where he was working over a groundwork provided by his studio, which led to the development of the extreme freedom and fluency which characterise his style after 1625.

Plate XVIII

Henry IV receiving the portrait of Marie de Médicis, 1622–25. Oil on canvas. 156¼ ×117 in. (394 ×295 cm.). Paris, Louvre.

The portrait of the future queen is presented to the king by Eros and Hymen. France, represented by a semi-nude figure, urges the king to enter into this alliance, which is approved by Jupiter and Juno, who appear seated on clouds. Near the king, two cupids, taking his helmet and shield, indicate the long peace which the marriage will bring to France.

Plate XIX

The portrait of Marie de Médicis (detail from Plate XVIII).

Plate XX

Marie de Médicis arriving at Marseilles, 1622–25. Oil on canvas. 156¼ ×117 in. (394 ×295 cm.). Paris, Louvre.

France and the city of Marseilles come before the queen to welcome her. Fame proclaims from the sky the happy arrival. In the foreground are marine deities.

Plate XXI   *The sirens* (detail from Plate XX).

The freedom and plasticity of this particular detail deeply impressed Delacroix, who made a copy of it. He notes in his *Journal*, apropos of a visit to see the pictures: 'Also the sirens never seemed to me so beautiful. Abandon and the most complete audacity alone can produce such impressions.'

Plate XXII   *Lot and his daughters fleeing from Gomorrah*, 1625. Oil on panel. $29\frac{1}{2} \times 46\frac{7}{8}$ in. (74.3 ×119 cm.). Paris, Collection of Ulysse Moussalli.

Rubens's depiction of the Biblical incident has much in common with the way in which the Bassani treated similar subjects. Similar frieze-like, rather straggling compositions turn up in a number of pictures by various members of this family. And the ass, with its load of carefully painted valuables, reminds us of the interest taken by the Bassani in just this kind of detail.

Plate XXIII   *The apotheosis of the Duke of Buckingham*, c. 1625. Oil on panel. $25\frac{1}{8} \times 25\frac{1}{8}$ in. (64 ×64 cm.). London, National Gallery.

George Villiers, first Duke of Buckingham (1592–1628), was the brilliant and arrogant court favourite of Charles I and James I. He exercised enormous influence over English politics, and in the first three years of Charles I's reign was the virtual ruler of England. He was at this period the advocate of an anti-Spanish policy, the keystone of which was, naturally enough, and Anglo-French alliance. In 1625 he paid a diplomatic visit to Paris to see how far he could depend on French assistence in furthering his aims. It was on this occasion, according to the evidence of Philippe Rubens, the artist's nephew, that the duke and Rubens met. Rubens painted a portrait of the duke and probably at the same time received the commission for a ceiling, for which this picture is the model. The ceiling itself was formerly at Osterley Park, Middlesex. Buckingham seems to have developed a strong taste for Rubens's works, for on his assassination in 1628 he owned thirty of them, including (in all probability) several illustrated in this book.

Here we see Rubens employing the motifs and formulae generally employed for such sacred subjects as the *Assumption of the Virgin*—only now they are pressed into service for purely secular purposes. We also see the first statement of themes which will appear again in the *Whitehall Ceiling* (see Plates XXVII–XXX).

The picture also offers evidence of Rubens's ability to assimilate influences from many sources. One of the heads in it is apparently derived from Carracci. It seems to be borrowed from a drawing which Rubens once made copying one of the preparatory studies for the Carracci decorations in the Palazzo Farnese.

Plate XXIV   *The hermit and the sleeping Angelica*, c. 1625–28. Oil on panel. 19 ×26 in. (48 ×66 cm.). Vienna, Kunsthistorisches Museum.

The subject of this little cabinet picture is drawn from the *Orlando Furioso* of Lodovico Ariosto (1474–1533). This poem is supposed to have been the inspiration of Spenser's *Faerie Queene*, which it in some respects resembles, and the painters of the seventeenth and eighteenth centuries were fond of painting incidents drawn from its picturesque and complicated narrative. Here Rubens picks on an incident to be found in Canto VIII, in which the heroine Angelica, carried off by magic to a desolate island, falls into the power of a wicked hermit:

In pious strains, with hypocritic air,
He now began to soothe the weeping fair;
While as he spoke, his roving fingers press'd,
Her alabaster neck and heaving breast;
Till, bolder grown, he clasp'd her in his arms:
But here, resentment kindling all her charms,
Back with her hand the feeble wretch she threw,
While every feature glowed with rosy hue.
Then from his scrip he takes, of sovereign use,
A little vial fill'd with magic juice;
In those bright eyes, where love was wont to frame
His sharpest darts, and raise his purest flame,
A drop he sprinkles that had power to steep
Her heavy eye-lids in the dew of sleep...

From the translation of John Hoole,
published in 1799

The picture is not only one of Rubens's most beautiful studies of the nude, it is also important as a forerunner of the painting of the French eighteenth centrury. It bears, for example, a strong resemblance to Watteau's *Jupiter and Antiope*, and a still stronger one to some of Fragonard's paintings of the nude.

The picture may be either the one which was listed in the inventory of Rubens's estate in 1640, or the one depicting the same subject which was in the Duke of Buckingham's collection.

Plate XXV   *Thomas, Earl of Arundel*, c. 1629. Oil on canvas. 26 ×20³/₄ in. (66 ×52 cm.). London, National Gallery.

Thomas Howard, Earl of Arundel (1586-1646), formed the first great collection of works of art in England. Horace Walpole says of him, in *Anecdotes of Painting in England*: 'The earl was not a mere selfish virtuoso; he was bountiful to men of talents, retaining some in his service, and liberal to all.'

On the other hand, Clarendon, Arundel's contemporary, appears to have disliked him, and gives an amusingly malicious account of his character in the *History of the Great Rebellion*: 'He was generally thought to be a proud man, who lived always within himself, conversing little with any who were in common conversation: so that he seemed to live as it were in another nation, his house being a place to which all people resorted, who resorted to no other place; strangers, or such who affected to look like strangers and dressed themselves accordingly... It cannot be denied that he had in his person, in his aspect and countenance, the appearance of a great man, which he preserved in his gait and motion. He wore and affected a habit very different from that of the time, such as men had only beheld in the pictures of the most considerable men; all which drew the eyes of most, and the reverence of many, towards him, as the image and representative of the primitive nobility, and native gravity of the nobles, when they had been most venerable; but this was only his outside, his nature and true humour being much disposed to levity and delight, which indeed were very despicable and childish.'

Rubens's depiction of Arundel's 'outside' tallies so exactly with Clarendon's description that there seems little doubt that the portrait must have been an excellent likeness.

Plate XXVI   *The triumph of Julius Caesar*, 1629–30. Oil on canvas. 35½ ×65 in. (90 ×165 cm.). London, National Gallery.

This is a free copy after one of the Mantegna cartoons now at Hampton Court. Rubens must have seen them at the time when he was negotiating the commission for the *Whitehall Ceiling*. It is interesting to see how Rubens has modified the Mantegna composition in the direction of greater movement and suppleness.

The picture was still in Rubens's possession at the time of his death.

Plate XXVII–   *THE WHITEHALL CEILING*
XXX   Rubens's correspondence shows that he was interested in providing decorations for Inigo Jones's new Banqueting House in Whitehall as early as 1621. He stayed at the court of Charles I in 1629 and 1630, and succeeded in getting the commission. When he returned to Antwerp he made a general plan of the whole scheme for the various compartments, and the canvases were finished by August 1st, 1634. The *Whitehall Ceiling* is the only great scheme of decoration by Rubens which still remains in its original position. The *Apotheosis* panel weighs $2^1/4$ tons.

Plate XXVII   *James I uniting the kingdoms of England and Scotland*, c. 1629–34. Oil on panel. 25 ×19 in. (63.5 ×48.3 cm.). Worcestershire, Private Collection.

This is an example of the preparatory studies which Rubens made for the ceiling. The *Esther and Ahasuerus* of Veronese, in San Sebastiano, Venice, seems to have inspired some details of the composition. The figure of the king leaning forward seems to be based on that of Veronese's Ahasuerus; and in the foreground is the figure of a warrior which is very like one in Veronese.

Plate XXVIII   *The apotheosis of James I*, 1629–34. Oil on canvas on panel. 384 ×246 in. (975 ×625 cm.). London, Banqueting House, Whitehall.

This large central compartment shows Rubens's talent for allegory at full stretch. Here abilities which for the most part had been put at the service of Catholics and the Catholic Church are pressed into the service of a 'heretic' government. Oddly enough, the terminology turns out to be no whit different.

Plate XXIX   *Genii with a garland and Genii with animals*, 1629–34. Oil on canvas on panel. 94 ×468 in. (239 ×1,190 cm.). London, Banqueting House, Whitehall.

These two friezes of children are among the most delightful of all Rubens's decorative inventions. Those with the garland symbolise the abundance prevailing in the time of James I, and those with animals, the peacefulness of the reign. Watteau copied these friezes—or more probably, he copied the designs for them which he found in the collection of his patron Crozat.

Plate XXX   *The bounty of James I triumphing over avarice*, 1629–34. Oil on canvas on panel. 216 ×94 in. (549 ×239 cm.). London, Banqueting House, Whitehall.

In complete contrast to the playfulness of the friezes is this simple, but magnificently weighty and monumental grouping of two figures. It reminds us that Rubens is known to have made designs for sculpture.

Plate XXXI   *Portrait of Hélène Fourment*, c. 1630–31. Oil on panel. 38¹/₄ ×26³/₄ in. (96 ×69 cm.). Munich, Bayerische Staatsgemäldesammlungen.

Rubens gives a very matter-of-fact account of his decision to marry a second time in a letter to Pieresc dated December 18th, 1634: 'I resolved to marry again, not yet being disposed to the austere celibate life, and reflecting that, while continence must be placed above everything, we may also seek legitimate pleasures, in thanking God for those He grants us. I have therefore married a young woman of honourable though bourgeois birth, though everyone urged me to choose a court lady. But I was afraid of finding my companion subject to pride, that chief vice of the nobility, especially among the women, and therefore I chose someone who would not blush to see me take up my brush. And, truly, I loved my liberty too much to exchange it for the embrace of an old woman.'

Despite these avowals, Rubens's pictures of Hélène have a special glow which it is hard not to attribute to his love for her. They also show the development of Rubens's art. This particular portrait, for example, shows much greater freedom of handling than the *Rubens with his first wife, Isabella Brandt* (Plate II) of twenty-one years earlier.

Plate XXXII   *The Flemish kermess*, c. 1630, though traditionally dated 1636–38. Oil on panel. 59 ×103½ in. (149 ×261 cm.). Paris, Louvre.

This picture, so abounding with energy and love of life, fully deserves the adjective 'epic' which, despite its comparatively small size, is so often applied to it. It is not, however, as fully spontaneous as might be supposed at first glance. Some of its ideas come from Peter Breughel the Elder, some from the German sixteenth-century print-makers, in particular from Hans Sebald Beham. Adriaen Brouwer, whose work Rubens is known to have admired, seems also to have contributed something. But a famous sheet of drawing of a dancing couple does show that much was taken, at white-heat and with unerring skill, from nature itself. A long descent of peasant scenes stems in large part from this work.

36

Plate XXXIII *The garden of love*, c. 1632–34. Oil on panel. 49½ ×68 in. (125 ×171.5 cm.). Aylesbury Waddesdon Manor.

An unfamiliar version of a famous composition. The picture is a later variant of the better-known one in the Prado, Madrid. It perhaps shows, grouped by families, the sisters and brothers-in-law of the Fourment family. The dancing couple (see Plate XXXIV) seem to be meant for Rubens himself and Hélène Fourment, while at the right is the woman represented in *Le Chapeau de Paille* (Plate XVII).

This picture is the predecessor of the *fête galante* pictures of the eighteenth century. Its stately good manners are in complete contrast to the wild abandon of *The Flemish kermess* (Plate XXXII).

Plate XXXIV *The dancing couple* (detail from Plate XXXIII).

Plate XXXV *The Adoration of the Magi*, 1634. Oil on panel. 129¼ ×97¼ in. (328 ×249 cm.). Cambridge, King's College.

A very important picture which recently returned to public view. It was commissioned by the White Sisters at Louvain in 1634, and Rubens was paid 920 florins for it before March 9th, 1634. The preliminary sketch is in the Wallace Collection.

This enormous picture is treated with the utmost freedom, perhaps because it was wanted in a hurry. There is a tradition, which Feynolds mentions, that it was painted in eight days. Its air of sketchiness, its very bravura, earned it stern censures from earlier critics. Reynolds calls it 'a slight performance'. The attitude in which the Virgin sits has also caused some carping. J. B. Descamps comments in 1760 in his *Voyage Pittoresque de la Flandre*, that though the composition is 'knowledgeable and full of finesse', he does not think the Virgin 'sits easily'. Reynolds says, 'The Virgin holds the infant but awkwardly, appearing to pinch the thigh.' But for modern eyes the main point and the main delight of the picture is the utter spontaneity with which the whole enormous expanse of canvas has been painted, the soft lustre of the thinly brushed colours.

Plate XXXVI *Head of the Negro king* (detail from Plate XXXV). Cf. Plates V and XVI.

Plate XXXVII *The rape of the Sabines*, 1635. Oil on panel. 66¾ ×92 in. (169.5 ×234 cm.). London, National Gallery.

The subject is taken from the accounts in Plutarch's *Life of Romulus* and Book I of Livy. Besides the interest current at the time in classical themes, the Mannerist and Baroque painters were encouraged to paint the rape of the Sabines for another reason—the great opportunity the subject offered for introducing complicated combinations of figures.

In Florence there was a famous group by Giovanni da Bologna; and Pietro da Cortona, one of the leading Italian Baroque artists, painted his version of the theme about 1630. Nicolas Poussin painted a *Rape of the Sabines* (now in the Louvre) which is just about contemporary with this one by Rubens. The Poussin and the Rubens make an interesting contrast. The Poussin is more learned—and more staccato. It does not have the sinuous, flowing movement of the Rubens. Nevertheless this picture is less violently Baroque than some of Rubens's earlier compositions.

Plate XXXVIII   *The judgement of Paris*, 1635–37. Oil on panel. 57^1/$_8$ ×76^3/$_8$ in. (145 ×194 cm.). London, National Gallery.

Painted for Cardinal Richelieu. The subject has fascinated painters at all epochs because of the opportunity it offers for depicting the nude. In this case, one can see even more clearly than usual how Rubens adopts a different canon of proportions for clothed and unclothed figures. Those unclothed are broader, fleshier, altogether more substantial. A comparison with the *Marie de Médicis arriving at Marseilles* (Plate XX) will show how much taller and slenderer Rubens's clothed figures are.

Plate XXXIX   *The Château de Steen*, c. 1635–37. Oil on panel. 54 ×92^1/$_2$ in. (137 ×234 cm.). London, National Gallery.

One of the most famous of Rubens's landscapes. Rubens only discovered the possibilities of landscape painting late in life. Previously he had left many of the landscapes in his pictures to be painted by specialists. The thing which seems to have impelled him towards the fullest possible exploration of the art of landscape was his love of the Château de Steen and the countryside around it. Steen lies near Malines. Rubens purchased the property in 1635.

Plate XL   *Landscape with a rainbow*, c. 1635–37. Oil on canvas. 54^3/$_4$ ×93^1/$_2$ in. (138 ×236 cm.). London, Wallace Collection.

This picture is the pendant to *The Château de Steen* (Plate XXXIX). Rubens was very interested in changeable effects of light—anything that would add to the air of freshness, of transitory beauty, which he was trying to catch. He was also fond of painting effects of sunset or early evening light.

Plate XLI   *Sunset landscape*, c. 1635. Oil on panel. 19^1/$_2$ ×32^7/$_8$ in. (49.5 ×83.5 cm.). London, National Gallery.

The Chateâu de Steen is in the middle distance.

Plate XLII   *Landscape with a tournament*, c. 1635–40. Oil on panel. 28^3/$_4$ ×42^3/$_4$ in. (73 ×108 cm.). Paris, Louvre.

One of the most mysterious of all Rubens's pictures—a kind of waking dream, half-fact half-fantasy. The nearest comparison is with some nineteenth-century Romantic picture with a chivalric subject, such as Chassériau painted.

Plate XLIII   *Hélène Fourment with her children*, c. 1636. Oil on panel. 44^3/$_4$ ×32^1/$_2$ in. (113 ×82 cm.). Paris, Louvre.

The children are Clara, Johanna and Frans. This beautiful picture, so utterly free that it is really no more than a large sketch, anticipates Renoir in a startling way, even to the attitudes which Hélène and her children take up. Renoir in fact made a copy of it.

Plate XLIV   *Landscape with a shepherd*, c. 1637. Oil on panel. 24½ ×37 in. (62 ×92 cm.). London, National Gallery.

A less realistic, more deliberately 'Arcadian' treatment of the landscape theme, which seems to hark back to Giorgione.

Plate XLV   *St Augustine*, 1637-38. Oil on canvas. 104¼ ×69½ in. (263 ×175 cm.). Prague, National Gallery.

Commissioned from Rubens by Countess Helena Martinitz, and put in position in 1639. St Augustine stands on the shore looking at the child Jesus who is playing there with a shell. Above flies an angel, who carries in one hand the mitre and crozier of a bishop, and in the other the heart which is St Augustine's symbol.

Plate XLVI   *The horrors of war*, c. 1637-38. Oil on paper on canvas. 19½ ×30¼ in. (49 ×76 cm.). London, National Gallery.

This is the model for the picture in the Palazzo Pitti, Florence. Rubens explains the allegorical programme in a letter dated March 12th, 1638 and addressed to the Antwerp painter Justus Sustermans who was then resident in Florence: 'The principal figure is Mars, who, leaving open the temple of Janus (whose doors were, according to Roman custom, kept shut in times of peace), strides with his shield and his bloodstained sword and threatens the people with disaster. He ignores Venus, his paramour, who, accompanied by cupids, tries by kisses and caresses to hold him back.

'On the other side Mars is drawn forward by the Fury Alecto who bears a torch in her hand. Monsters at her side signify Plague and Famine, the inseparable companions of War. On the ground lies a woman with a broken lute, who signifies Harmony which is incompatible with War, also a woman with a child in her arms, to show that Fecundity, Maternity and Charity are opposed by War, which destroys all things. There is, too, an architect lying with his instruments in his hand, signifying that that which is built in times of peace for the convenience and ornament of a city is laid in ruins and overthrown by the force of arms. There should also, I believe, be found on the ground, between the feet of Mars, a book and several drawings on paper, to indicate that he tramples on literature and other liberal arts. There ought to be, furthermore, a bundle of arrows, with the cord that bound them undone—these, when bound together are the emblem of Concord. Thrown beside them are a caduceus and a branch of olive, emblems of Peace. The woman in mourning, clothed in black and with her veil torn, and stripped of her jewels and ornaments, is unhappy Europe, afflicted for so many long years by rapine, outrage and misery, beyond expression harmful to everyone. Her attribute is the Globe, upheld by a little angel or genius, and surmounted by a cross, which denotes the Christian universe.'

The picture shows Rubens reverting to a preoccupation which he shared with the great Venetians—the contrast between nude flesh and the hardness and metallic sheen of armour. Earlier examples of this preoccupation occur in the *Crowning of the Hero* of about 1612 at Munich, and in the *Triumph of the Victor* of about 1614 at Cassel.

Plate XLVII *The triumphal chariot of the victory of Calloo*, 1638. Oil on panel. $40^3/_4 \times 28$ in. (103 × 71 cm.). Antwerp, Museum of Fine Arts.

An example of the other commissions which Rubens undertook, besides straight-forward commissions for pictures, is this model for a triumphal chariot designed for the purpose of commemorating the victory won by the Cardinal-Infant Ferdinand over the Dutch, at Calloo on 21st June, 1638. The town of Antwerp commissioned the chariot from Rubens in the same year, and it appeared, from 1640 on, in the annual *ommegang* (procession) at Antwerp. Rubens had executed earlier commissions of this kind for the city, including a series of triuphal arches erected in the streets for which other sketches survive. On the left of this sketch is the plan of the floor of the chariot.

Plate XLVIII *Hélène Fourment with a fur cloak*, c. 1638–40. Oil on panel. $69^1/_2 \times 38$ in. (175 × 96 cm.). Vienna, Kunsthistorisches Museum.

This painting is without doubt the most intimate of all Rubens's pictorial expressions of his love for his second wife—at once tender and powerfully sensual. It is not in the least idealised; such details as the feet deformed by the wearing of tight shoes betray that this is indeed a real woman. Nor is the drawing satisfactory from the academic point of view—Hélène's legs are not satisfactorily related to the upper part of her body, and the cloak masks an impossible junction. Nevertheless, of all Rubens's multitudinous works, this is possibly his masterpiece. The picture was the one thing which Rubens specifically left Hélène in his will.

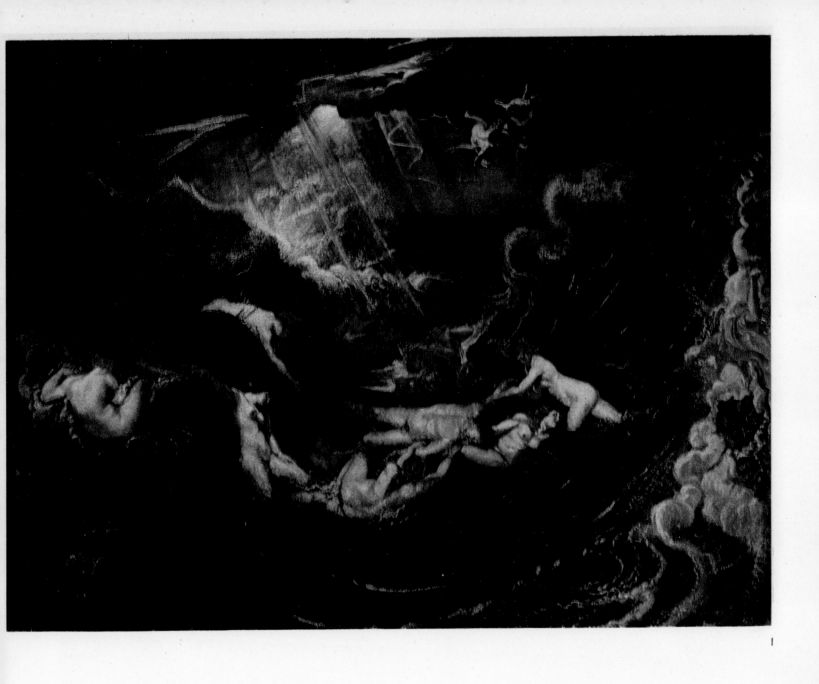

III

IV.

X

XII

XIV

XV

XVI

XVII

XXI

XXII

XXIV

XXVI

XXXI

XXXII

XXXIII

XXXVI

XXXVII

XXXVIII

XXXIX

XL

XLI

XLII

XLIV

XLVI

XLVIII